Why do we have?

RIVERS AND SEAS

By Claire Llewellyn
Illustrated by Anthony Lewis

HAMLYN

Contents

First published in Great Britain in 1995 by
Hamlyn Children's Books, an imprint of Reed Children's Books Limited, Michelin House,
81 Fulham Road, London SW3 6RB, and Auckland, Melbourne, Singapore and Toronto.

Text copyright © 1995 by Claire Llewellyn
Illustrations copyright © 1995 by Anthony Lewis

ISBN 0 600 58691 X

A CIP catalogue record for this book is available at the British Library.

Editor: Veronica Pennycook
Designer: Julia Worth
Consultant: Pat Pye, Ginn & Company Ltd

Printed and bound in China

A Busy River

Big rivers are lively places. Watch one for a while, and you'll see pleasure boats cruising to and fro, and cargo ships returning to port.

The river too is on the move. Its journey started a long way from the city, and has already taken several days.

Where a River Starts

Rivers start on hilltops and mountain peaks. Here, there is so much rain and snow that water is always trickling down the hillside.

One tiny trickle leads into another. Slowly, they grow into a stream of clear, fresh water that picks up speed and flows quickly on its way.

Faster and Faster

As the bubbling streams flow into one another, the river grows bigger and gathers pace. It races down the hillside, snatching up small stones and pebbles. They swirl around in the water, chipping away at the banks and river bed.

Over thousands of years, this pounding and chipping carves a valley into the hillside.

The river flows very quickly

The River Slows

By the time it reaches the bottom of the hill, the river has joined up with others, and is larger still.

On the flatter ground, the river becomes calmer, wider, deeper. It flows along much more slowly. Instead of racing over obstacles, it now sweeps round them, making big bends called meanders.

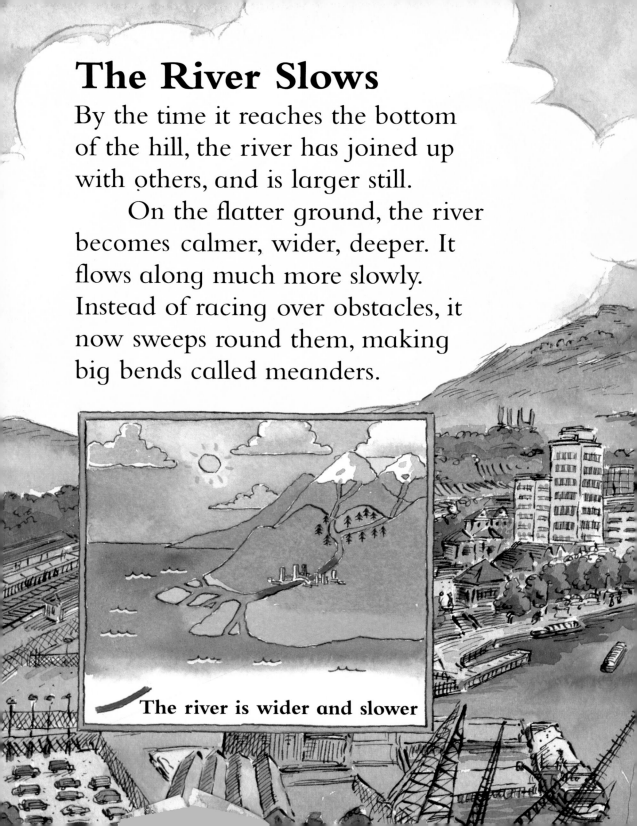

The river is wider and slower

Journey's End

The river ends its journey at the sea. By now, it is moving so slowly that the mud and stones it was carrying sink down to the river bed, and pile up into mudflats. The gooey mud is teeming with snails, shellfish and wriggly worms – a delicious feast for seabirds!

The river's mouth

The Salty Sea

Not far from the river's mouth lies the open sea. The air is fresher here, with the tangy smell of salt.

The sea is vast. It stretches much further than our eyes can see. Twice a day it rises up the beach, and then it falls – leaving a tangle of seaweed and sticks on the high tide line.

Under the Sea

Along the coast, dry land slopes down into the sea. The water here is shallow, light and warm. Colourful fish hide in the seaweed and dart among the rocks.

Far out from the shore, the seabed slopes down steeply. The water is deeper, cold and dark, with fewer plants and animals.

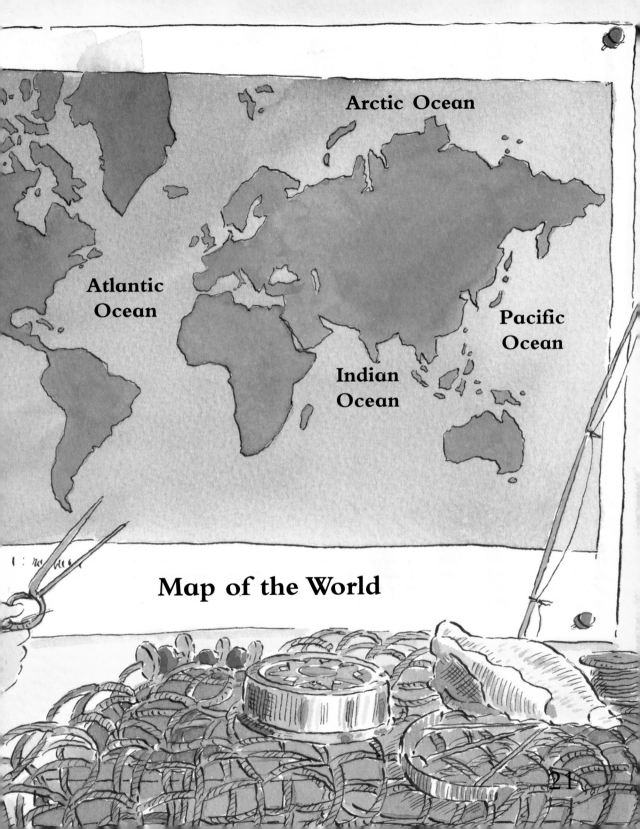

Arctic Ocean

Atlantic
Ocean

Pacific
Ocean

Indian
Ocean

Map of the World

The Water Cycle

The oceans play an important part in the world's weather. The Sun's heat makes water evaporate from the sea. As the water vapour rises in the sky, it cools, and forms clouds. Their rain feeds the rivers that flow to the sea.

The world's water moves in a never-ending circle from the land and sea to the sky. We call this the water cycle.

Water evaporates

23

Index